*A Search-Equilibrium Approach
to the Micro Foundations of Macroeconomics*

The MIT Press
Cambridge, Massachusetts
London, England

A Search-Equilibrium Approach to the Micro Foundations of Macroeconomics

The Wicksell Lectures, 1982

PETER A. DIAMOND

© 1984 by The Massachusetts Institute of Technology

All rights reserved. No part of this book may be reproduced in any form by any electronic or mechanical means (including photocopying, recording, or information storage and retrieval) without permission in writing from the publisher.

This book was set in Mergenthaler Linotron 202 Sabon by DEKR Corporation and printed and bound by Halliday Lithograph in the United States of America

Library of Congress Cataloging in Publication Data

Diamond, Peter A.
  A search-equilibrium approach to the micro foundations of macroeconomics.

  (The Wicksell lectures; 1982)
  Includes bibliographical references.
  1. Economics—Mathematical models.
2. Equilibrium (Economics).
3. Search theory. 4. Macroeconomics—Mathematical models. 5. Microeconomics—Mathematical models.
I. Title. II. Title: Micro foundations of macroeconomics. III. Series.
HB141.D43 1984   330'.0724   84-9704
ISBN 0-262-04076-X

To Kate

The Wicksell Lectures

In 1958 the Wicksell Lecture Society, in cooperation with the Social Science Institute of Stockholm University, the Stockholm School of Economics, and the Swedish Economic Association, inaugurated a series of lectures to honor the memory of Knut Wicksell (1851–1926). Until 1975 lectures were given each year. After a period of dormancy the series was reinaugurated in 1979 by the Swedish Economic Association. Starting with the 1982 lectures, a set of lectures will be offered every two years.

Contents

LECTURE 1

A Formal Search Model   1

LECTURE 2

The Uses of Search Theory   33

References   65

Author's Note

I am grateful to the Swedish Economic Association and the Stockholm School of Economics for the opportunity to give these lectures and for their hospitality during my very enjoyable stay in Stockholm.

Some of the material in lecture 2 was presented in the Frank Paish Lecture to the Association of University Teachers of Economics at Loughborough, England, in 1981.

I am grateful to my colleague Peter Temin for valuable comments in preparing these lectures and to the National Science Foundation for supporting the research reported here.

A Search-Equilibrium Approach to the Micro Foundations of Macroeconomics

LECTURE 1

A Formal Search Model

Following the publication in 1970 of the Phelps volume, *The Microeconomic Foundations of Employment and Inflation Theory*, "the micro foundations of macro" has become the name of a well-defined branch of economic theory. The name is somewhat misleading. If macroeconomics is to acquire a firm microeconomic basis, we will at the same time have changed microeconomics to incorporate the macro reality of cyclical unemployment, which is now missing in general-equilibrium micro models. Thus, a better title for my two lectures would be *A Search-Equilibrium Approach to the Integration of Micro- and Macroeconomics*.

Search theory played a basic role in many of the studies in the Phelps volume and has continued to be important in subsequent research. I want to start by underlining the difference between my use of search theory and that in the earlier literature. Most writers apply search theory to the labor market, while implicitly or explicitly closing the model in the familiar general-equilibrium way; that is, a Walrasian auctioneer clears all markets. Of course, the auctioneer is a fiction. My starting point has been to build a model that avoids any such mechanism, a model that does not assume a frictionless, costless, perfect re-

A Formal Search Model

source allocation device. (For a more detailed analysis of the steady-state model presented here, see Diamond 1982a.)

My alternative assumptions are that all trades in the economy take place between two individuals, rather than between an individual and "the market," and that it is time-consuming to locate a trading partner. The fact that it may be costly in resources as well as time (which has been explored in the partial-equilibrium search literature) will be ignored for the sake of simplicity. Thus, I will present a general-equilibrium search model, rather than a partial-equilibrium search model embedded in a general-equilibrium Walrasian model. The focus of this study is, then, the problems for an economy that come from the difficulties in coordinating trade and the implication of these difficulties for aggregate production decisions.

The Walrasian auctioneer performs two functions: the matching of buyers and sellers and the calculation and announcement of equilibrium prices. I will use a search technology to replace the frictionless matching of the Walrasian auctioneer—that is, I will assume that individuals must spend time to locate someone with whom to negotiate over the possibility of trade. I will preserve the second role of the Walrasian auctioneer, however, by inaccurately assuming correct forecasts of future prices and rates of trading opportunities. Since everyone predicts accurately, all trades will take place at equilibrium prices. By making only one change in standard assumptions, I can focus on the implications of costly coordination. This single change, however, causes major changes in the results.

I will proceed in these two lectures by first presenting a simple, formal model. By exploring in detail the equations and the geometry of this model, I hope to bring out the basic difference between thinking in this way about the allocation of resources and thinking in terms of a Walrasian auctioneer. In my second lecture I will step back from the formal model and relate my approach to the existing literature. To look ahead for a moment, I will criticize the policy of constant monetary growth on the basis that the natural rate of unemployment is not unique and that macro policy should therefore attempt to direct the economy toward a desirable unemployment rate.

Before launching into the formal model, I want to give an overview of its key mechanisms and central results. The main feature of a general-equilibrium search model is the explicit description of the technology for the coordination of trade. It seems to me a plausible assumption—and a critical one for the conclusions to follow—that the trade technology exhibits in-

A Formal Search Model

creasing returns to scale. That is, if more people are attempting to trade, it becomes easier to carry out trades. I will be modeling this in a barter setting, but, as I will indicate later, the basic results and insights will carry over to a monetary setting.

Given the central role of the assumption of increasing returns to scale, I want to consider the question of its plausibility. The model I will present is a steady-state equilibrium model. It has that form primarily for its simplicity. But I am interested in the model as a description of phenomena that are important in the context of a business cycle and must therefore evaluate the appropriateness of the assumption to an economy that is subject to cycles.

In modern Western economies, trade in both the consumer and labor markets is coordinated through a large number of separate shops and marketing agents. Associated with this trade is a large quantity of capital in place as well as a great deal of knowledge and experience in individual trading patterns. Over the business cycle, as the volume of trade varies, we find increasing returns as trade varies more than either fixed capital or inventory levels. These increasing returns would be plausible even if we believed that the trade technology showed constant returns across steady states. The fact of spatial dispersion may well imply increasing returns to scale even in the latter context. But it is the cyclic context that is important here and that makes the assumption of increasing returns plausible.

Given these aggregate increasing returns, there is a trade externality associated with increased inventory available for trade. When individuals add to the stock of inventories, they make it easier for other individuals to locate potential trading partners. This externality, which has been explored in detail in the partial-equilibrium literature (Diamond and Maskin 1979, 1981; Diamond 1981, 1982b, Mortensen 1982a, 1982b), plays a central role in the general-equilibrium discussion that follows. Because of this trade externality, equilibrium will not be efficient in the absence of government intervention. It is difficult to envision cost-effective private devices for internalizing the externalities caused by the availability of one trader to the universe of potential trading partners.

Moreover, this externality involves a positive feedback: increased production for inventory makes trade easier; easier trade makes production for inventory more profitable and therefore justifies its increase. This positive feedback with an externality implies the possibility of multiple equilibria. In the models I will present, additional plausible assumptions on the technol-

A Formal Search Model

ogy will imply the necessity of multiple equilibria whenever the economy has an equilibrium with a positive level of production. With multiple steady-state equilibria, there are multiple equilibrium paths for some initial positions. I will argue that this property of an economy is important for thinking about macro policy.

The multiple equilibria here are different from those in a Walrasian model. There, it is common to have multiple equilibria, but given suitable assumptions, all of them are Pareto optima. Later in this lecture I will present a simple example with two equilibria where one equilibrium Pareto dominates the other—where every agent in the economy will prefer the path leading to a high level of production over the path leading to a low level of production. This distinction seems to me to be critical in relating the model to the problems we associate with business cycles. This type of feedback and externality linkage is not new in the economics literature. A similar idea lies behind the analysis of underdevelopment in terms of cumulative processes rather than simple equilibrium (see, for example, Myrdal 1956).

For simplicity, the model I will present has no money and no credit; all transactions are barter transactions. Because of this simplification there is no role for interest rates, and the linkage of the ideas here with Wicksellian ideas must await future development of this model. There is also no hired labor. I am therefore claiming that it is possible for a barter economy of self-employed individuals to have business cycles. Obviously this model leaves out many of the elements that are important in shaping modern business cycles. The purpose of the simple model is to illuminate the role of imperfect trade coordination, a factor that would be harder to see in a more complete, more realistic model.

In a barter economy the key link between production and the profitability of production comes from the availability of inventories for barter. In a monetary economy with hired labor the link between production and the profitability of production has different elements. Among them is the fact that the payment of wages before the sale of output represents a shift in purchasing power that plays an important role in aggregate demand. This element is, of course, missing in the simple barter model I will present.

I must mention one severe limitation of the model. Obviously a barter model cannot address the problems associated with inflation; in addition, the monetary economies I have developed have not been set up to incorporate inflation. That is

A Formal Search Model

part of a conscious research plan: inflation and unemployment are both such difficult problems to understand that it is good strategy to model each of them separately before attempting a model that will address both of them at once.

In a barter economy inventories play a central role. I assume that there is a single good in this economy. Then I can refer to the stock of inventories as a scalar rather than a vector. In order to preserve the critical function of trade, I add to the assumption of a single good the further restriction that no individual can consume what he himself has produced. Thus, all output must go through the trade process after being produced. This simple structure is meant to capture what is important for macroeconomics about the advantages of specialization and production for the market. I denote by e the stock of inventories available for trade. The model has continuous time. Thus we are interested in the aggregate flow rate of meetings between potential trading partners at a time when the aggregate stock of inventories is e. Since I assume that each unit of inventory is associated with a single trader attempting to peddle that unit, I also refer to e as the number of workers employed in the trade process. When aggregate inventories are e, I write the rate of contacts of potential trading partners as $eb(e)$. To begin with, I assume that all of these contacts lead to trade and that the negotiation process is instantaneous; thus the rate of change in the stock of inventory as a consequence of trade is $-eb(e)$. Later I will introduce an element of differentiation among goods that will lead to the possibility that two potential trading partners do not carry out a trade after meeting. I am assuming increasing returns to scale; therefore I assume that $b(e)$ is strictly increasing in e.

This describes the aggregate transactions technology. We also need a consistent description of the individual experience. The length of time that goods are in inventories (or, in the case of industries that work on back orders, the length of time to delivery) is stochastic. We therefore want to model the individual arrival of trading opportunities as a stochastic process. The simplest stochastic process is a stationary Poisson process; that is, in any interval of time of given length, the probability of the arrival of a trading opportunity is the same. Thus, for each individual, the parameter of the Poisson process, which gives the arrival rate of potential trading partners, is b. Adding up over individuals, the aggregate arrival rate is eb, which is taken to be determinate, not stochastic. Competitive behavior is that in

A Formal Search Model

which individuals think of b as a parameter and do not recognize the relationship between b and the aggregate stock of inventories. This is analogous to price-taking behavior in the Walrasian model.

To complete the story of the dynamics of inventory accumulation, we need the determinants of the flow of goods into inventory. A simple approach is to assume that each agent not engaged in trade is engaged in production. There are then $n - e$ individuals engaged in production. I also model the production process as a Poisson process, since this is a simple way of getting single units of inventory produced. Then, a production opportunity is the opportunity to produce a single unit of the good for inventory, with different opportunities differing in their costs. I denote by $G(c)$ the cumulative probability distribution of the labor disutility cost of producing a unit of inventory. Whenever an opportunity arrives, the individual makes an independent draw from $G(c)$ to determine the cost of that particular project. Once he knows the cost, the individual decides whether to carry out the project or whether to wait for a better opportunity. This is better viewed as a waiting model than as a search model; it bears some relationship to search unemployment, which for many people consists of waiting for an opening in one's particular field.

The dynamics of inventory accumulation is shown in equation 1, where c^* is the cutoff level of cost and a the arrival rate of production opportunities:

$$\dot{e} = -eb(e) + (n - e)\, aG(c^*). \tag{1}$$

That is, individuals accept all projects that cost less than c^*. The cutoff cost, c^*, is the analogue of the reservation wage.

In figure 1, I have plotted the pairs of the stock of inventories, e, and the cutoff costs, c^*, that will result in a stationary level of inventories. In drawing the figure I have assumed that there is a minimum cost $\underline{c}$ on any project. Thus, with a cutoff cost less than $\underline{c}$, the only steady state is at a zero level of inventories. Above $\underline{c}$ the curve $\dot{e} = 0$ is upward sloping, since a greater willingness to invest goes with a greater number of traders if the flows into and out of inventories are to match. There is a maximum sustainable stock of inventories associated with taking all opportunities; it is the solution to equation 1 with $G(c^*) = 1$. I have drawn the curve asymptotic to that level under the assumption that there is no limit to the cost of projects.

A Formal Search Model

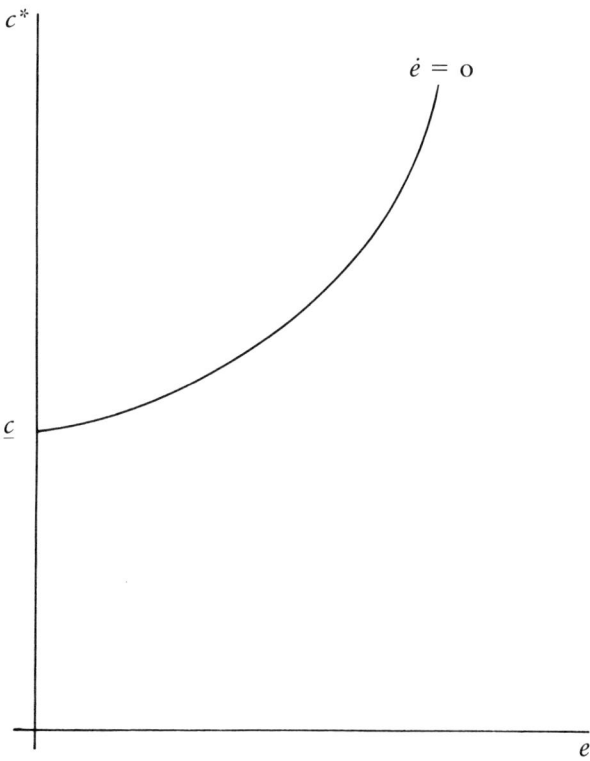

Figure 1

That seems to me to be an honest reflection of the capabilities of the human mind to think up ever more costly projects.

The next step in the analysis is to consider the determination of c^*, the individual willingness to act on production opportunities. I will start by analyzing this for an economy in a steady-state equilibrium; that is, where individuals know the parameters of the economy and know that the parameters are not changing. An individual who knows a and b chooses c^* to maximize expected lifetime utility. Individuals experience a circular process, first looking for a production opportunity, next looking for a trading opportunity, and then looking again for a production opportunity. Completion of a production project generates a labor cost, which is a draw from $G(c)$; completion of a trade transaction generates a utility of consumption, which I denote by y and which I assume, for the present, is not random and is independent of the past history of consumption and labor. I also assume that individuals have a constant subjective utility discount rate, which I denote by r.

A simple way of modeling individual choice is by dynamic programming methods. I will denote by W_e the expected discounted lifetime utility for an individual who currently has a unit of goods in inventory; by W_u, the expected lifetime utility

A Formal Search Model

for an individual who does not have a unit of goods in inventory. By assumption, an individual with goods in inventory either does not learn of additional production possibilities or has such large inventory carrying costs that he does not want to have more than one unit in inventory; these are the only two states an individual can be in. The dynamic programming setup in a steady state is just like the asset value approach: the rate of discount on utility times the value of being in any position is equal to the expected flow of benefits from being in that position. If one has inventories, the flow probability of something happening is b, and what happens is utility from consumption, y, plus the capital loss from having traded away inventory, $W_u - W_e$. In the event of being unemployed, one is waiting for the arrival of a production opportunity. That happens with flow probability a. When it happens, the individual chooses all opportunities that cost less than c^*, and each of them gives a disutility c and a capital gain as the individual moves back to having a stock of inventory. Thus,

$$rW_e = b(y + W_u - W_e)$$

and

$$rW_u = a \int_0^{c^*} (-c + W_e - W_u) dG(c).$$

(2)

The optimal cutoff cost is precisely equal to the capital gain from a change in position; that is, the maximization of the integral in equation 2 is achieved by taking every opportunity that raises expected lifetime utility:

$$c^* = W_e - W_u. \tag{3}$$

Solving equations 2 and 3, we get c^* as a function of b and thus of e, the aggregate stock of inventories, since b is a function of e. That is shown in figure 2, where I have added $c^*(e)$ to figure 1. $c^*(e)$ starts at the origin, since there is no flow of trading opportunities when there are no potential trading partners. $c^*(e)$ is bounded above by the utility y, since, at positive interest, it cannot pay to produce something at a cost exceeding its consumption value. The curve is increasing and, in this simple version, also concave, provided b is a concave function of e.

I have drawn the figure with three intersections (including the one at the origin).[1] It would be possible to have only one

---

1. With naive expectations the middle equilibrium is unstable and the other two are stable.

A Formal Search Model

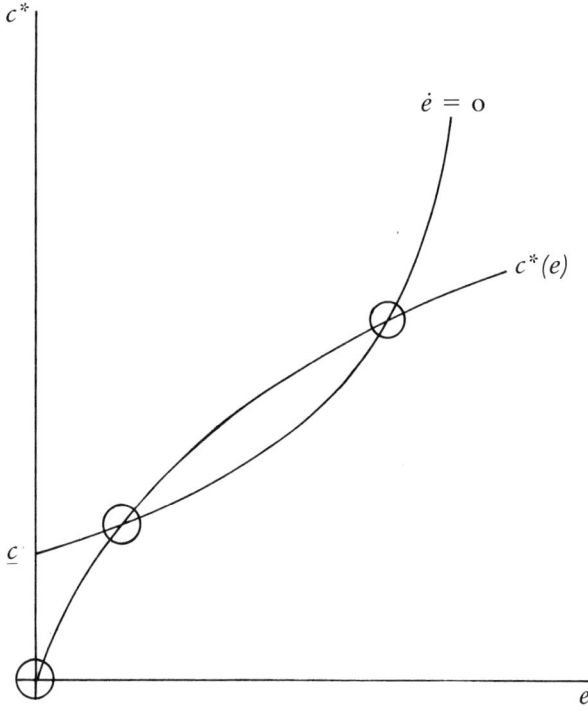

Figure 2

intersection, which would represent a shutdown of the trade economy. As a knife edge the economy could have two equilibria. As long as the economy has an equilibrium with a positive level of production, it will have multiple equilibria. It could have many more than the three I have drawn. Since neither $b(e)$ nor $G(c^*)$ need have particularly nice properties, there is no reason for restricting ourselves to three equilibria. Thus I have demonstrated that an active economy with this trading technology has multiple equilibria.

It is clear from the technology that there is an externality involved. Even the equilibrium with a high level of production is not efficient. Welfare would be higher if everyone were willing to undertake slightly more costly projects. Moreover, the expected utility of each individual would be higher, not just the summed utility.[2] By the envelope condition, a small increase in the willingness to invest at the individual optimum has, in itself, no effect on individual utility. But the combination of many such decisions increases b, the arrival rate of trading opportunities, and so makes everyone better off.

---

2. I am grateful to K. Judd for bringing this further result to my attention.

A Formal Search Model

Consider the following two generalizations of this model. First, what happens if carrying out a production opportunity also involves coordination between agents? In order to generate two units of inventory, assume that one needs two workers to carry out a project, with the cost the same to each of them. In that case a in equation 1 is a function of the available stock of unemployed workers rather than a parameter. The economy now has two externalities. Additions to inventory generate an increase in the ability to carry out trade and a decrease in the ability to find coworkers to carry out production opportunities. There is no reason for these offsetting externalities to balance precisely. The economy has the possibility of overemployment, which seems to me to be realistic: there is the possibility of such a low level of frictional unemployment that it becomes too expensive to fill vacancies. The question of the optimal steady state or, more interesting, of the optimal path for the economy, then involves the idea of the optimal level of employment; the solution might entail going to a lower level rather than a higher level of employment.

In a second generalization, I want to introduce the idea of matching in tastes when two traders come together. Instead of the utility of consumption always being y, let us assume that the utility of consumption is a random draw from the cumulative probability distribution $H(y)$. The draw is the same for both trading partners. Thus, we can continue the idea of all goods being ex ante identical and still have a matching problem in trading. The effect of this change is to introduce a second decision into the model, that of the cutoff level of utility that just makes worthwhile the depletion of inventory. If y^* is that cutoff level of utility, then $1 - H(y^*)$ is the fraction of potential trades carried out, and the inventory change equation becomes

$$\dot{e} = -eb(e)\,[1 - H(y^*)] + (n - e)\,aG(c^*). \tag{4}$$

Analyzing the optimal choice of y^*, along the lines used to analyze the choice of c^*, we get the condition

$$c^* = y^* = W_e - W_u. \tag{5}$$

That is, the individually optimal utility cutoff for carrying out a trade, and so depleting inventory, is precisely equal to the individually optimal cutoff on production cost that just makes it worthwhile to add to inventory. This naturally follows from having a single shadow price on the stock of inventory.

A Formal Search Model

The foregoing analysis yields a result that runs counter to the presumed advantages of increasing aggregate demand. The externality in the model runs from the stock of inventories to the ability to trade, with a greater stock of inventories making it easier to trade. A greater willingness to carry out trade is a decrease in y^*. Decreasing y^* tends to lower the stock of inventories in the economy, making trade more difficult. Thus the external economy comes from being less eager to trade. That is, with the economy in a steady-state equilibrium, welfare improvement comes from increasing c^* and y^* together, making people more willing to produce and less willing to trade (given inventories).[3] To explore the relevance of this peculiarity, one would want to model more realistically the sources of actual demand.

---

3. Combining this extension of the model with the previous one, which makes a a function of $(n - e)$, one can calculate the sign of the effect on aggregate welfare of raising the equilibrium levels of the cutoff cost for production or the cutoff benefit for trade. The sign of this derivative is the same as the sign of

$$eb' \int_{y^*}^{\infty} (y - y^*)dH(y) - (n - e)a' \int_0^{c^*} (c^* - c)dG(c).$$

This very simple model of trade and trade externalities has been criticized on occasion for the lack of individual control variables to affect individual ability to trade. In modern economies, agents seeking to trade advertise, build up links with regular trading partners, and develop reputations for offering good deals. If the model were generalized to bring in all of these elements, it would still be true that, at the optimal level of these control variables, an increase in the availability of potential trading partners would raise the profitability of engaging in the trade process. Thus, I believe the externality and multiple equilibria that I have described are robust to realistic extensions of this very simple model of the way people seek out trading partners.

I will turn now from steady-state analysis to a non-steady-state example in order to bring out the critical role of expectations (Diamond and Fudenberg, forthcoming). This is an important aspect of the model, since the combination of a critical role for expectations and multiple equilibria will open up a particular perspective on the potential for macroeconomic policy. For simplicity, let us assume now that all projects cost exactly the same, c. Thus there are two possible simple states of the economy, namely, the state where everyone takes all production

A Formal Search Model

opportunities and the state where no one takes any opportunity.[4]

In the analysis that follows, an *optimist* is someone who believes that everyone else will take all production opportunities; a *pessimist* is someone who believes that no one else will produce. These views will be contrasted with the naive view that the arrival rate of opportunities will not change. Someone with naive views has a willingness to invest, $c_n^*(e)$, which is simply the function $c^*(e)$ analyzed earlier. In figure 3, I have redrawn $c^*(e)$, now labeled $c_n^*(e)$. An optimist believes that the economy is on the path for $\dot{e}$ given by equation 1 with $G(c^*)$ equal to 1. Given that belief, an optimist has a willingness to produce that is a function of the level of inventories. In figure 3, I have drawn the optimist's willingness to produce as $c_o^*(e)$. The optimist is more willing to produce than the person with naive expectations when he sees the level of inventories rising toward the equilibrium level, since he believes that trading opportunities

---

4. This makes the curve $\dot{e} = 0$ a step function, giving precisely three equilibria for y sufficiently large. I ignore the middle equilibrium where some of the (identical) production opportunities are taken and some are not.

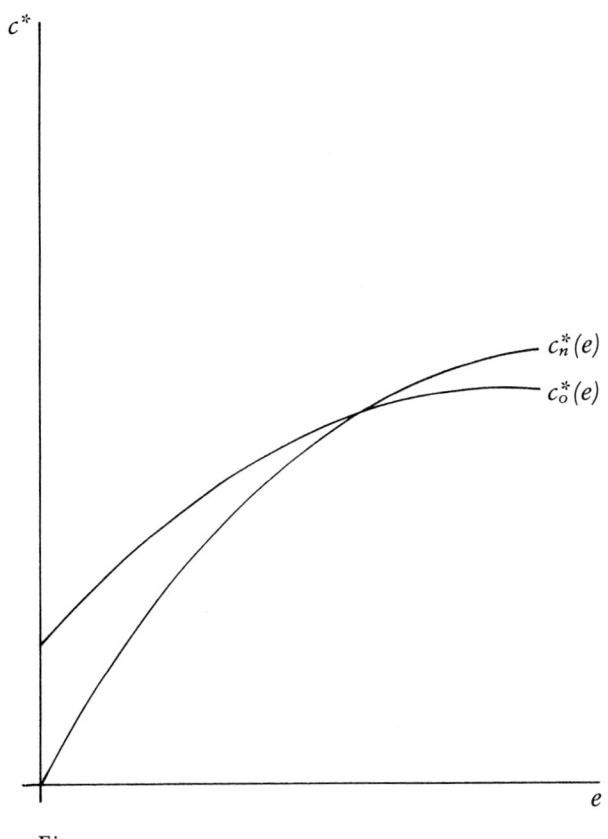

Figure 3

will come more frequently in the future. The optimist has a lower willingness to invest when he sees inventories declining toward the equilibrium level. A pessimist believes that $\dot{e}$ is negative and that the economy is converging toward the shutdown equilibrium. Adding the willingness to invest of the pessimist, $c_p^*(e)$, to figure 3, we have figure 4.

In figure 4, I have also drawn a horizontal line at the actual level of the cost of production, c. An individual will invest when his cutoff cost is at least as large as c. The intersections of the horizontal line at c with $c_o^*(e)$ and $c_p^*(e)$ divided the e axis into three regions. To the left of e_o the stock of inventories is so low that even an optimist is unwilling to produce. In that case the only rational-expectations equilibrium for the economy has only pessimists and is convergent to the origin; the economy collapses to self-sufficiency. If the aggregate stock of inventories is larger than e_p, even a pessimist is willing to produce. In that case the only rational-expectations equilibrium has only optimists and is convergent to the high-employment equilibrium. Between e_o and e_p both types of convergence represent rational-expectations equilibria. If everyone is a pessimist, all will find their pessimism justified as the economy collapses. If everyone is an optimist, again all will find out they are right as the economy

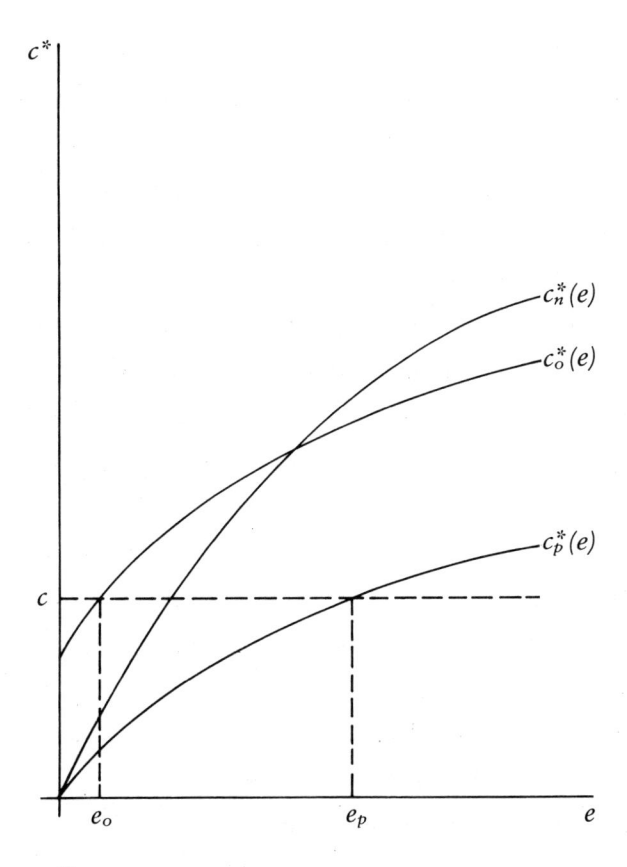

Figure 4

A Formal Search Model

converges to the good equilibrium. For an initial position below the long-run steady state, along the optimistic path inventories grow, as does the incentive to produce. Along the pessimistic path the stock of inventories shrinks, as does the incentive to produce. Here is the cumulative process I mentioned earlier. On the optimistic path trading opportunities are higher at every moment than on the pessimistic path. Thus, every individual is better off on the optimistic path than on the pessimistic path, and we have Pareto comparability of these two different equilibria.

In this context rational expectations is obviously an incomplete theory of expectations. It does not select one of these two paths for the economy. For a more complete theory we need to learn how people actually form their expectations. This is especially important in a setting where widespread initial optimism would be confirmed by events, as would widespread initial pessimism. I am not aware of well-developed theories of expectation formation that are applicable to such a setting.

With multiple equilibria there is an important potential role for government. The government can attempt to influence beliefs by suggesting that there is nothing to fear but fear itself. More important, the government can take fiscal action to increase aggregate demand and so launch the economy on the optimistic path. In this way we can model pump-priming while being completely consistent with individual maximization and rational expectations. The basis for this possibility is that more production makes production more profitable. One can go beyond this simple discussion of alternative paths to develop a cycle model: with suitably timed waves of optimism and pessimism, one can have a rational-expectations cycle.

As a final generalization of this class of models, I will briefly describe how the model can be changed from a barter to a monetary economy (Diamond 1984). I denote by e, as before, the stock of inventory, with one individual for each good in inventory. And I denote by m the stock of real money holding, with one individual holding enough money to buy one unit of the good. I assume an aggregate transactions technology $f(e,m)$ that tells us the flow rate of meeting between would-be buyers and would-be sellers, when the stock of inventories is e and the stock of real money in the hands of people out shopping is m. This is the analogue to $eb(e)$ in the barter model. Similarly, I will assume that $f(e,m)$ shows increasing returns to scale and is otherwise a well-behaved function. Individuals now go through a three-step process. They produce for inventory, sell inventory for money, and then search for a supplier from whom to buy.

A Formal Search Model

After consuming, they start the process over again. The individual-choice problem is a straightforward generalization of the one described in the barter model.

To close the model, we need a rule for the price level. The price level then determines the stock of real money, given the stock of nominal money. Since I want to model price determination on the basis of individual trade, I have chosen to close the model with the assumption (which is the Raiffa bargaining solution) that, in equilibrium, the stocks of inventory and of real money are such that the gain to the seller from having money rather than inventory is precisely equal to the gain to the buyer from having a unit of the commodity to consume rather than a unit of real money. That is, buyer and seller split evenly the gain for completing a trade. In the notation used above, extended to include W_m as the expected lifetime utility of someone having a unit of money, $W_m - W_e$ is the gain for the seller and equals $y + W_u - W_m$, the gain to the buyer:

$$W_m - W_e = y + W_u - W_m. \tag{6}$$

This solution is sensible in a setting of symmetric bargaining between buyer and seller, which is an uncommon marketing situation in modern times. I did not want to model the more common pricing by the seller on a take-it-or-leave-it basis, because of my desire to stay close to the Walrasian model and to avoid certain modeling complications.

Given this equation to close it, the monetary model has the same basic properties as the barter model. An economy that has an equilibrium with a positive level of production will have multiple equilibria. None of the equilibria is efficient relative to allocations achievable by changes in both the willingness to produce and the stock of real money. Across equilibria, those with a higher level of production have a higher velocity of money and lower prices, nominal money stock held constant. Thus, the economy has the appearance, not of sticky prices, but of perverse prices. High levels of output are associated with low prices. I have not extended the model to analyze non-steady paths; therefore I cannot yet claim that a monetary policy, in the form of distributing money to the unemployed, for example, will move the economy from a poor equilibrium onto the track headed for a better equilibrium. That possibility remains to be studied.

As a model of the workings of a monetary economy, this one is severely limited by the lack of credit, which is an important partial substitute for money. Developing models with credit

A Formal Search Model

lies in the future. But it is worth pointing out that credit has the same kind of feedback mechanism as does the production and trade process I have described. When an individual is considering whether to provide credit, he looks ahead to the possibility of his own future credit needs before the loan is repaid. The more optimistic an individual is about the future availability of credit to himself, the more willing he is to provide credit to others. So we have the same sort of link as before and we would expect multiple equilibria in the level of credit in the economy. These equilibria in turn are likely to interact with the feedback mechanism on the production side. Thus, in a model of an economy with credit, the government's role in keeping up credit availability may be similar to the role I have assigned it here in keeping up the profitability of production.

This lecture has been formal, focusing narrowly on a particular way of perceiving the trade coordination difficulties in a large, diversified, specialized economy. I think I have learned something about the workings of actual economies from my exploration of the problem of logically combining individual maximization, correct perceptions of the economic environment, and this way of describing the trade process. In particular, I have described models with multiple natural rates of unemployment and so have suggested a need for an active policy to pursue the most desirable of these. Next I will contrast what I have learned from search models with other writings on the micro foundations of macro.

LECTURE 2

The Uses of Search Theory

Having presented a specific simple model of search equilibrium, I will devote this lecture to making the case that a search framework is a promising one for an integration of micro- and macroeconomics. I will compare search equilibrium with the rational-expectations approach to business cycles pioneered by Robert Lucas (1972; Lucas and Sargent 1981); I will also discuss the compatibility of the search-equilibrium approach with attempts to find a micro basis for the sticky prices and wages that characterize the Keynesian approach (Azariadis 1975; Baily 1977). As part of the general case for the importance of search theory, I want to begin by presenting two microeconomic problems—consumer prices and the duration of unemployment—that are very hard to fit into a simple, classical market setting and for which a search approach seems appropriate.

One of the implications of a classical market model of consumer transactions is the law of a single price. In equilibrium all transactions take place at the same price. In the United States, and, I imagine, in most other decentralized economies, casual experience shows that the law of a single price does not hold if a market is defined as a set of different stores that a single consumer is likely to visit. This casual empiricism has been supported in a study of consumer prices in the Boston area by Pratt, Wise, and Zeckhauser (1979). They selected thirty-nine commodities at random from the *Yellow Pages* of the telephone directory, and a research assistant telephoned all or many of the stores listed as selling those products. Some of the products were standardized or specific brands and so homogeneous; others were services and not homogeneous. In the working paper, but not, alas, in the published version, the actual distributions of prices are reported for all thirty-nine commodities. Examining them, one can calculate that in seventeen of the thirty-nine cases the ratio of the highest price to the lowest price is at least two to one. Lest one think this is strictly a phenomenon of outliers, a reexamination of the list, striking either the highest or the lowest price, whichever brought the ratio down further, still left ten of the thirty-nine with a ratio of at least two to one. Nor are the high ratios restricted to the nonhomogeneous commodities in the sample.

A study of supermarket pricing (Brown and Oxenfeldt 1972) has brought out clearly the lack of vector ordering across supermarkets of the prices of various commodities. Dividing the commodities in the supermarket into four classes of goods, the authors found that twenty-three of the twenty-nine supermarkets had above-average prices in one department and below-average in another. This irregularity in differences complicates the problem of effective shopping. My own experience includes frequent purchases of paper diapers. I regularly visit a supermarket and a drugstore that share a parking lot and carry the same brands. The diapers are consistently cheaper in the supermarket by approximately one dollar (seven dollars as opposed to eight). I should add that on average the supermarket is slightly quicker to shop in.[1] I imagine that the raw data used by the Bureau of Labor Statistics in the construction of the Consumer Price Index would yield a similar pattern of considerable price disparity despite the highly competitive settings of many sellers and buyers.[2]

---

1. That the two stores are part of the same corporation may possibly be part of the appropriate model of price setting but is not relevant for the conclusion that consumer shopping behavior results in sufficient sales at both prices to sustain this pricing behavior.

---

2. Standard Metropolitan Statistical Area maximum and minimum gasoline prices have been made available. See Marvel 1976, which also cites earlier empirical analyses of gasoline price distributions.

The Uses of Search Theory

One could attempt to torture these data into a classical market setting by distinguishing many markets, losing thereby the simplicity and the power that are the virtues of a classical market framework. In contrast, it is very easy to frame search models that result in equilibrium distributions of prices—even, in some circumstances, with symmetry among firms. Thus, a researcher interested in understanding the distribution of consumer prices would do well to leave the market setting and use a search setting instead.

By and large, research in this area has been theoretical, not empirical. Two properties have come out of the theoretical research. First, even when the market settles down to a uniform price, it is unlikely to be the classical competitive price. The reason for this is clear. If it takes an effort to gather information about prices, then stores that have succeeded in communicating with specific shoppers have at least a little bit of monopoly power over their potential competitors. (This is clearest when a shopper visits stores to receive price information.) Lots of little bits of monopoly power tend to interact and can raise the price by more than just a little bit. In an extreme version—with symmetry, no price reputations, and limited information flows—arbitrarily small search costs compound so much as to result in the collusive monopoly price without any collusion (Diamond 1971). A sufficiently small price difference from other stores loses no customers in this model. Thus, the uniform price equilibrium can only occur if firms choose not to raise prices even though they do not fear the loss of customers to other stores—that is, at the monopoly price. This extreme result is implausible in more general information settings (including, for example, advertising and price reputations) but highlights the power of even small amounts of friction to add up to large differences in the nature of equilibrium. This same model of search and pricing can also be used to determine the rate of convergence of prices to equilibrium. In other words, when consumers gather price information by shopping, past prices affect consumer beliefs about prices elsewhere and so affect the demand curve for any particular supplier. This generally affects optimal price setting. In consequence, transactions take place at disequilibrium prices, if we define equilibrium as involving stationary prices.

The second property revealed by the theoretical research is the possibility of generating an equilibrium distribution of prices. This possibility arises naturally with differences among stores (Reinganum 1979), which are a natural consequence of geographic differences. Even in the symmetric case one can generate distributions of prices. This can occur with sampling by individuals that results in their receiving prices sometimes one at a time and sometimes several at a time. Then, both high-price-low-volume and low-price-high-volume strategies can yield the same profits with suitable numbers of stores of each type. This result was derived by Butters (1977) and has been very nicely clarified by Burdett and Judd (1983), who bring out the significance of sampling stores only one at a time—which gives the uniform monopoly price—as opposed to sampling stores in varying numbers—which gives a nondegenerate price distribution. Even in a symmetric case where prices are sampled one at a time, one can have a distribution of prices. Salop and Stiglitz (1982) linked up intertemporal demands in a model with no ex ante differences among consumers except the dates they enter the market. Young shoppers purchase for two periods when they find a low-price store, while purchases for a single period are made in all other cases. In this way there can be equal profits at two different prices. Axell (1977) constructed a striking example by having a suitable distribution of search costs in the population. The lesson I want to draw here is that there are real-world situations where the cost and difficulties of coordinating trade make for large differences in the nature of equilibrium, both in theory and in practice, compared to the prediction of the classical competitive model. There is no reason to think these micro facts are irrelevant for macroeconomics.

The empirical analysis of the determinants of the distribution of durations of spells of unemployment presents another occasion for using a search approach (Clark and Summers 1979; Lancaster 1979; Nickell 1979). The literature analyzes the flows into and out of unemployment, concentrating on the important policy question of the effect of unemployment compensation on these flows. The essential assumption in these models is that the development of employment possibilities is viewed by the individual as stochastic. Casual empiricism suggests that this is indeed the way individuals see the economic environment and that it is not merely a result of the problems faced by econometricians. Again, this question does not fit naturally in a model using a classical frictionless labor market. The evidence from the micro data suggests that the labor market needs to be thought of in terms of a sequential process that will

The Uses of Search Theory

be subject to the same coordination difficulties as the general-equilibrium model I presented in the first lecture.[3]

After these partial-equilibrium examples of the use of search, I turn to a general-equilibrium example. Most writings in monetary theory that consider equilibrium without business cycles fall into one of two groups. Some papers are focused on long-run growth and recognize money primarily as a store of value and therefore as a part of individual portfolios. The central focus of these models is the effect of different levels of money or different levels of inflation on capital accumulation and government revenue. The second group of models, the group I will discuss, addresses the role of money in providing liquidity. Some of these models focus on the advantages of money over barter; others, on the implications of varying amounts of liquidity in a monetary economy. Analyses of the optimal quantity of money for liquidity purposes are examples of this group of models.

If one is to analyze explicitly the role of money in transactions, one must have a transactions technology that relates ei-

---

3. A third appropriate topic for search analysis is the workings of the housing market. For examples, see Daniel, Kornai, and Weibull 1981; Loikkanen 1982.

ther resource use or the completion rate of transactions to the stock of money being employed for transactions purposes. One approach to this question is exemplified by a paper by Grandmont and Younes (1973). Using a discrete time model, they assume that some fraction of monetary receipts within a period can be used for purchases in the same period, while money held at the start of the period is needed for any purchases above this level. Thus, consumers have a budget constraint and a finance constraint. A difficulty with this approach is the problem of deciding the appropriate way to model the finance constraint. One necessarily focuses on transactions happening within a period to justify the choice of constraint. If one is to approach this formally, one ends up analyzing the detailed pattern of transactions, and the concept of a period no longer plays a role in the model. Also, the correct length of the period for the purpose of analysis is itself endogenous, since individuals control the organization of transactions.

The monetary model described at the end of the first lecture is a continuous-time model and, it seems to me, the right sort of model to use for addressing this question. Either money or credit or goods for barter must be available for an individual to transact, so a more complicated version of that model would examine the margins at which transactions take place in each of these three forms. In analyzing these margins, one would be examining the effect of the availability of different quantities of money on the rate of completing transactions. To close the model, one would consider the feedback of the rate of transaction completion to the rest of the economy. The simple case presented in the last lecture had only money; there was neither credit nor barter. By explicitly formulating a transactions technology relating the rate of meeting for transactions purposes to the numbers of individuals with money and with inventories, the model brought out clearly this role of money. More complicated models would not restrict money holdings to the level just needed for purchasing a single unit and would at the same time focus on the individual's choice whether or not to convert money into less liquid, higher-yielding assets.

Until an equilibrium model is developed that has both money and less liquid assets, and that has transactions technologies both in the asset market and in the goods market, one cannot think rigorously about the role of money in terms of open-market operations, or about the role of banking in generating liquidity in the economy. Given the difficulties in formulating the appropriate constraints in a discrete-time model, I suggest that the type of continuous-time model I presented earlier is a sensible starting place for thinking about the liquidity role of money. I also suggest that models focusing on money's role as a store of value (such as recent overlapping-generations models) are incomplete bases for thinking about monetary policy if they lack considerations of liquidity.

This brings me to my central argument, the usefulness of a search-equilibrium approach in the integration of micro- and macroeconomics. I will proceed in four steps. First, I will discuss the use of equilibrium analysis; second, I will contrast the assumption of classical markets with that of search; third, I will consider pairwise trading with ongoing relationships rather than spot transactions with the market; and fourth, I will discuss rational expectations.

To contrast with equilibrium models, I will start with a strawman Keynesian model. Prices and wages are given. Resources are allocated on the basis of these prices and a rationing mechanism. Prices and wages then adjust in response to the presence of rationing and past inflation rates. We can see that this model is not micro based: transactions are occurring at prices that neither clear the market nor come from an explicit micro source that might generate trade at non-clearing prices;

furthermore, price adjustment is not related to any explicit consideration of self-interested price setting or price negotiations. Nevertheless, a model based on this approach can be developed to give a reasonably good fit to aggregate time series data. In addition this is a simple framework that can readily be used for macro problems and policies.

There are at least two possible reasons for constructing micro-based models as an alternative to this approach. One is a belief that the Keynesian model is basically wrong. The second is a belief that the model can be improved by reconstruction from a micro foundation. The former is represented by the rational-expectations equilibrium approach to business cycles; the latter by my search-equilibrium approach. There is a problem of vocabulary here. The model I presented in the first lecture has rational expectations, is an equilibrium model, and can be viewed as an alternative to the Keynesian model; yet it is not the type usually referred to as a rational-expectations equilibrium model. Such a description is usually applied to the models pioneered by Lucas, which I refer to as the classical market approach.

The classical market approach says that the economy may have the appearance of slow, nonclearing price and wage movements, but that actually markets clear. The combination of small price and wage movements and large output and employment movements is due to large intertemporal substitutabilities and misperceptions of relevant relative prices. Such misperceptions are necessarily present when markets are incomplete; that is, observed nominal prices are not adequate guides to intertemporal relative prices. Note that market clearance and market nonclearance are mutually exclusive views of the world.

On the other hand, my search model had production for future transactions. Those transactions were modeled as having flexible prices, in the sense that no meeting giving rise to an advantageous trade opportunity resulted in a failure to complete the trade. A change in the basis of transactions is compatible with the production and search model. Thus, the framework could readily be modified to have some trade possibilities passed over because of commitments to particular prices based on explicit contracts or maintenance of long-run relationships.[4] Simi-

---

4. Even without this element, negotiation with limited information will result in a failure to complete all deals that are mutually advantageous. See, for example, Fudenberg and Tirole 1983.

larly, the price determination rule for completed transactions could be somewhat historically determined rather than a bargaining solution. Presumably, such changes in the model would compound the economic difficulties and the need for good policies. Thus, the two equilibrium approaches have very different relationships to Keynesian analysis: clearing markets are incompatible with it, while a search approach is compatible without necessarily surrendering its micro foundation.

Having decided to explore an equilibrium approach to macro, one still has a range of choice over the type of equilibrium. I will contrast classical market equilibrium with search equilibrium, although some recent theoretical work has looked to monopolistic competition for new insights into macro (Hart 1982), and actual industry structures are likely to be important in a more fully developed search theory.

How does one decide whether competitive markets or search represents a better starting point for theoretical macro analysis? How does one decide whether existing classical market models or search models form a better basis for policy recommendations? We have two separate questions here because, like medicine, economics is concerned both with present problems and with the basic research that may help solve future problems. These two questions need not be given the same answers. Policy advice should be based on as accurate a picture of the economy as one has. Basic research is sometimes best done with assumptions that are known to be wrong: untrue assumptions may be chosen to isolate the workings of a particular institution or merely out of tractability.[5] For example, in microeconomics, one regularly analyzes *one at a time* the implications of assumptions other than those that will result in competitive equilibria being Pareto optima. For policy one needs to combine several such studies, even though basic research is best done with separate analyses. Since there are many things to be learned about the economy, the analogy of looking under the light for a key lost elsewhere is a bad one. There is no single key. On the other hand, it is very tempting to confuse assumptions chosen for basic research with true statements about the world. It is easy to forget that the tasks of basic research and policy advice are different. Just because a model was the right one to use for a particular question in basic research, it is not necessarily the right

---

5. All assumptions are untrue. Here I mean assumptions that are chosen even though they are less accurate than available alternatives.

one for a different question in basic research or for a related policy analysis.

Returning to the question of choosing between these different definitions of equilibrium, there are three related bases for choice. One is the fit to micro data (or stylized data). The second is the fit to macro data. The third is the robustness of the important findings to the more questionable assumptions.

From the micro perspective, the evidence I have already cited on price distributions and stochastic lengths of unemployment is a powerful indication that a classical market view is wrong and a search view is closer to being right. Modifying the market view to have many markets, with unemployment when one moves between them, as has been done by Lucas and Prescott (1974), would not seriously change this comparison, since movement among competitive markets would not generate the suitably stochastic duration of unemployment. Nor would this explain the sharp difference between the labor market experience of individuals who get laid off and that of individuals who do not. With voluntary search among clearing markets, expected utility would be equal for two equivalent workers at the same location who differ only in that one of them chose to seek work elsewhere.

This does not really settle the issue, however. The model I presented in the first lecture looks a great deal like the classical market model if one removes the assumption of trade externalities. That is, if the relative availability of trading partners does not affect the length of time to find a trade, then the search model behaves much like a classical market model. In the barter economy there is a unique efficient equilibrium.[6] In a labor market the absence of externalities would correspond to the relative availability of vacancies not affecting either the length of time to find a job offer or the quality of job offers. Casual empiricism strongly supports the search version that is not equivalent to a classical market model; but the comparison is less clear-cut than would appear without this equivalence.

The next basis for choice is the empirical fit with business cycle facts. The clearest statement of these appeared in a paper by the late Arthur Okun (1980). One major fact is the length of business cycles, or, alternatively, the extent of persistence of upturns and downturns. I am inclined to think that the classical

---

6. Shutdown of the economy is still an equilibrium, but the production cost cutoff function is discontinuous at the origin, making that equilibrium uninteresting.

market approach could be suitably adjusted to accommodate persistence, although this has not yet been satisfactorily done. A second important fact is that quits move cyclically while unemployment moves countercyclically. If the primary basis of unemployment is misperceptions on the part of workers, it is curious to find this divergence in behavior between employed and unemployed, with the employed supplying more labor (quitting less) while the unemployed are supplying less labor (staying unemployed). I think this divergence is likely to be an insurmountable problem for an equilibrium model based on clearing competitive markets. It ceases being a puzzle if the central vehicle for the business cycle is a change in the perceived shadow value of inventories (corresponding to c^* in the first lecture). This change could come from a failure of output markets to clear after macro shocks or from the sort of trade coordination mechanism described in the first lecture. A third fact is the difference across sectors of the economy in the size of price and wage movements. It was Okun's belief, and is the basis of much Keynesian thought, that this difference is important to the business cycle and can be explained by the differences across sectors in the nature of long-run relationships. Within the classical framework one can construct reasons for differential movements across sectors in the prices and wages needed to clear markets. It remains to be seen whether the classical approach to these facts will be as attractive as the disequilibrium reasons cited by Okun. Recent work has considered one further major puzzle for the classical market approach—that consumption is cyclical while leisure (measured as time not working) is countercyclical (Mankiw, Rotemberg, and Summers, forthcoming; Barro and King 1982). This is a central fact of business cycles. If one thinks of both output and labor markets as clearing, one has to work hard to develop a mechanism that explains why workers behave so differently in these two markets, consuming less when they take more leisure. The question is not whether a model with this property is conceivable. Rather, the question is whether the model is believable from the point of view of policy and whether, from the point of view of basic research, a model that has been built to solve these puzzles will be useful for solving new ones.

I come now to the third issue in choosing between models, namely, robustness. Even though one knows that the classical market assumption is not true, it might be satisfactory to proceed with building models based on that assumption. After all, any model is necessarily untrue. From the point of view of basic research the classical model has the two virtues of simplicity and familiarity: it permits an insightful analysis of new phenomena by making possible the isolation of new effects. The insights acquired from such a model can only be used as a basis of policy if the policy implications coming from the model are robust with respect to the assumptions we know to be untrue. To test validity for this purpose, one needs to develop alternative models to test the robustness of the prime policy conclusion of the classical market approach, namely, the limited power of macro policy. From the fundamental theorem of welfare economics, we know that in noncompetitive models the economy will frequently be inefficient in the sense that there are potential policies that can improve resource allocation efficiency. The issue at hand, however, is whether available macro policies can improve welfare in the presence of the specific imperfections thought to be important for a business cycle setting.

Sargent and Wallace (1975) have made an exploration of this type, examining the robustness of the ineffectiveness of policy to alternative formulations of the model. In their setting they find that ineffectiveness is robust provided rational expectations are preserved. In contrast, in my first lecture I showed that ineffectiveness was not robust to the change to a search setting with a trade externality. The prime elements of difference between the two settings are the trading externality itself, which is missing in a simple market model, and, more important, the implied multiple equilibria. Yet it is worth noting that multiple equilibria are a regular finding in infinite-horizon rational-expectations growth models (this is one of a number of insightful criticisms of the policy ineffectiveness result found in Shiller 1978) and so are not specific to search models. However, the growth models with multiple equilibria have not been linked up with cyclical questions.

I have argued that search models fit stylized micro data better than classical market models do. By pointing out the limitations of classical market models, I have suggested that search models may be capable of a better fit to macro data. Finally, I have argued that the prime policy recommendation coming from the classical market approach is not robust to some plausible modifications of the model. This seems to me to add up to a strong case for the search approach. I turn now to two issues in modeling that are compatible with a search approach: long-run relationships and not-necessarily-rational expectations.

In market models, individuals are conceived as trading with the market. There are no particular individuals on the other side of the market with whom they trade. Although a few markets do work this way, the bulk of transactions in Western economies are pairwise, with identifiable traders on each side of the transaction. In addition, many of the transactions in consumer markets, intermediate goods markets, and labor markets involve people who deal with each other repeatedly. This fact is the centerpiece for the attempt to construct the micro foundation for Keynesian macro out of implicit contracts (Azariadis 1975; Baily 1977). It is also central for models containing explicit long-term contracts that then give monetary policy real effects despite rational expectations (Fischer 1977; Phelps and Taylor 1977). The evidence of individual experience makes clear that pairwise trading is a more accurate description than trading with markets. Further, there is empirical evidence suggesting that repeated dealings make a difference. For example, it has been found that repeated dealings play a role in firms' decisions whether to sue after a breach of contract (Macaulay 1963); for a discussion of relationships, see also MacNeil (1974).

It seems to me that the proponents of contract approaches for modeling the labor market are right in arguing that wages are set in recognition of long-term relationships,[7] and that Okun (1981) was right in arguing that the same is widely true in consumer goods markets. The likelihood that both of these views are true and important for the design of policy implies that any policy recommendations from models without these views should be modified in the direction of simple fixed-price models. What has been lacking in this approach to macroeconomics has been a suitable framework to generate business cycles based on these facts. It seems to me that a sensible approach for basic research is to extend equilibrium models of transactions (including the one I employed in the first lecture) to include long-run relationships, with their concomitant informational asymmetries and bargaining difficulties. Thus the search approach can be complementary to the implicit contract, long-term explicit contract, and, more generally, disequilibrium price literatures. I have chosen to ignore these elements in my work to date both for the sake of simplicity and in order to make clear that trade coordination, in and of itself, is a source of policy conclusions that differ from those produced by classical market models,

---

7. Large firms and unions are also obvious micro realities that are important for the actual shape of business cycles.

even without the compounding factors of price and wage rigidity.

We come next to the assumption of rational expectations. Rational expectations is sometimes portrayed merely as the attempt by individuals to do the best they can with the information at hand or with their opportunities to gather information. In formal analysis, however, rational expectations has been modeled as correct knowledge of the structure of the economy together with accurate assessment of probabilities about random variables.

As a theory of expectation formation, rational expectations is obviously not complete. For one thing, it does not pick out a single equilibrium in a setting of multiple equilibria such as that described in the first lecture. For another, there is no model of learning, even though no one believes that people leap instantly to a correctly specified model of their environment when that environment changes. Presumably, learning theory, combined with a more detailed model of information and opinion flows, will pick out an equilibrium from the multiple equilibria. Much attention has been addressed to the question whether, in an economic environment where the parameters are endogenous to the beliefs about the economy, a sensible learning model will converge to a rational-expectations equilibrium ("Symposium on Rational Expectations" 1982). That exercise provides a useful way of learning about the implications of learning; but the acceptability of rational expectations does not stand or fall solely on the answer to the question.

In addition to being incomplete, it is my belief that rational expectations is basically incorrect.[8] There is a sizable literature by psychologists examining systematic mistakes in individual judgment and decision making in a stochastic environment, based on an analogy with the systematic mistakes people make in visual judgment (Kahneman, Slovic, and Tversky 1982; Nisbett and Ross 1980). In most settings people use decision-making devices that are effective; it is precisely because of this that they are led astray in other environments. Thus, systematic mistakes in one setting are consistent with the general view of rational expectations, once one incorporates human limitations. Brown and Oxenfeldt (1972) compared shopper perceptions of relative supermarket prices with the researchers' own pricing of

---

8. For a survey of rational-expectations models, including empirical tests, see Shiller 1978.

a particular market basket. They found that, as well as being affected by actual prices, price perceptions were strongly affected by store characteristics that plausibly belonged in a theory of supermarket pricing. While it is a sensible shortcut for consumers to rely on simpler facts that correlate with low prices, such reliance will lead to some errors. As of now, little has been done to incorporate these findings into economic theory, but that is not a basis for believing that rational expectations models are correct.

My belief that rational expectations is not an accurate description of the economy has several implications. For policy recommendation, it implies disbelief of the proposition that systematic policies have no effect. In basic research, on the other hand, the assumption of rational expectations is still the right assumption to use for most, but not all, analyses. In any model one would like to know how many of the results come from other mechanisms being modeled and how many of the results come from the expectations-formation assumption. We have organized much of microeconomic theory around the Walrasian model, understanding one by one the implications of deviating from the assumptions that make competitive equilibrium Pareto optimal. Similarly, in the macro area it seems to me to make sense to focus on particular problems in a rational-expectations setting and also to look at the implications of expectation errors. Obviously the question of errors becomes most important when we get to models that focus on turning points in business cycles.

Consistent with the rational-expectations framework has been the argument that one should focus on government policy rules, not individual government actions (Lucas 1981). That is, if the government is responding in a systematic way in its attempt to improve the economy, then, implicitly or explicitly, the government is following a policy. Individuals will react to the consequences for the economic environment of such a policy and, possibly, to the simple existence of such a policy. This observation is insightful and important and shows up in many discussions of the behavior of the postwar economy.[9]

---

9. For example, Solow (1978) has suggested that the downward price rigidity that has characterized the postwar United States in contrast with earlier periods is probably connected with the great decrease in output volatility in the American economy.

The Uses of Search Theory

It is often further suggested that one should look at policy rules in a rational-expectations setting (Lucas 1981). This is an inadequate framework for government policy for several reasons. First, this approach considers only long-run issues (Friedman 1978; Tobin 1980). Even though expectations are changing in the short run, and even though learning theory has been of little help in building macro models with stable parameters, one can reasonably believe that useful short-run policy can be designed in some settings, and so this possibility should not be ignored. Second, in the presence of multiple equilibria and inadequate understanding of the determinants of the choice between them, short-run actions, even experimental ones, may sometimes be the right government choice. This leads directly into my third point, that no one has the right model for the economy in either the short run or the long run.[10] Thus, one can have only limited

---

10. In the long run the economy does not settle down to a determinate state. Thus, it seems to me inappropriate to argue from determinate models, such as those with a known rate of inflation. Also, the economy will probably never settle down to a known stationary probability distribution, making long-run stationary equilibria of limited use for policy analysis.

faith in any model and, probably, less faith in long-run models that are not tied to what is known of the present. It is very likely that events will occur the possibility of which was not recognized at earlier times when models were built for long-run policy. Credit cards and electronic money may be examples of such events; they would have affected the success of a policy of steady monetary growth. The limited accuracy of existing models weakens the economic case for commitments to policy rules (whether feedback rules or not) and strengthens the argument that there are times when it is appropriate to focus on short-run actions—for example, when the parameters of long-run models are particularly unstable.

If one rejects having only long-run considerations, one can still accept the premise that one should consider the long-run implications of repeated applications of short-run policies.[11] But this premise leads to a basic difficulty. The problems encountered in designing models for short-run policy are different from

---

11. A second implication of this framework is the need to examine existing institutions to see whether institutional changes might result in a better economic framework, given available policies.

those encountered in designing models to describe likely distant-future states of the economy. In the current state of economics, short- and long-run issues are probably best approached by using fundamentally different models, with different simplifying assumptions. As for the problem of making policy recommendations, I suspect that the best way to proceed is by checking the short-run consequences of actions or policies in the best short-run models and by checking the long-run consequences in the best long-run models. Policy can then be based on the (somehow) combined answers. I believe that this approach will yield better policies than optimization of a single model, whether short-run, long-run, or hybrid.

The ideas of search have played two roles in the development of economic theory. One has been to clarify the implications of limited information in a basically static setting. Here the focus has been on the implied deviations from competitive-equilibrium pricing. Second, search has represented one way of modeling the fact that the resource allocation process takes time and is difficult to coordinate. Both of these elements are important for the actual workings of the economy and, I have argued, present a more realistic picture of modern Western economies than is the picture that comes from the assumption of classical markets. In addition, I have argued that the search approach represents a promising basis for thinking about price and wage stickiness.

I want to conclude by drawing out what I think to be the most important implication of the work I have done so far. The revolution or counterrevolution associated with equilibrium business cycles has relied heavily on the concept of a natural rate of unemployment. That has been the basis for arguing for severe limitations on the potentiality of successful policy and, at least in the United States, for arguing that policy making should be hamstrung. A premise of my work is that it would be difficult to make sense of cyclical unemployment unless one had a model that included frictional unemployment. That is, a model with a zero natural rate of unemployment would have shortcomings as a model of the business cycle. When I constructed a model that had frictional unemployment in it, at least with the assumptions I have employed, I found multiple natural rates of unemployment. The importance of this basically different way of viewing the world is that it shifts the presumption from the limitations on policy to the potential for good policy.

References

Axell, B. 1977. "Search Market Equilibrium." *Scandinavian Journal of Economics* 79:20–40.

Azariadis, C. 1975. "Implicit Contracts and Underemployment Equilibria." *Journal of Political Economy* 83:1183–1202.

Baily, M. 1977. "On the Theory of Layoffs and Underemployment." *Econometrica* 45:1043–1063.

Barro, R., and R. King. 1982. "Time-Separable Preferences and Intertemporal-Substitution Models of Business Cycles." University of Rochester. Unpublished.

Brown, F. E., and A. R. Oxenfeldt. 1972. *Misperceptions of Economic Phenomena*. New York: Sperr and Douth.

Burdett, K., and K. Judd. 1983. "Equilibrium Price Dispersion." *Econometrica* 51:955–969.

Butters, G. 1977. "Equilibrium Distributions of Sales and Advertising Prices." *Review of Economic Studies* 44:465–491.

Clark, K., and L. Summers. 1979. "Labor Market Dynamics and Unemployment: A Reconsideration." *Brookings Papers on Economic Activity*, 13–60.

References

Daniel, Z., J. Kornai, and J. Weibull. 1981. "A Model Framework for Analysis and Simulation of Housing Markets." Working paper, Department of Mathematics, Royal Institution of Technology, Stockholm.

Diamond, P. A. 1971. "A Model of Price Adjustment." *Journal of Economic Theory* 3:156–168.

Diamond, P. A. 1981. "Mobility Costs, Frictional Unemployment, and Efficiency." *Journal of Political Economy* 89:798–812.

Diamond, P. A. 1982a. "Aggregate Demand Management in Search Equilibrium." *Journal of Political Economy* 90:881–894.

Diamond, P. A. 1982b. "Wage Determination and Efficiency in Search Equilibrium." *Review of Economic Studies* 49:217–228.

Diamond, P. A. 1984. "Money in Search Equilibrium." *Econometrica* 52:1–20.

Diamond, P. A., and D. Fudenberg. Forthcoming. "An Example of Rational-Expectations Business Cycles in Search Equilibrium." *Journal of Political Economy.*

Diamond, P. A., and E. Maskin. 1979. "An Equilibrium Analysis of Search and Breach of Contract, I: Steady States." *Bell Journal of Economics* 10:282–316.

Diamond, P. A., and E. Maskin. 1981. "An Equilibrium Analysis of Search and Breach of Contract, II: A Non-Steady-State Example." *Journal of Economic Theory* 25:165–195.

Fischer, S. 1977. "Long-Term Contracts, Rational Expectations, and the Optimal Money Supply Rule." *Journal of Political Economy* 85:191–205.

Friedman, B. 1978. "Discussion" in *After the Phillips Curve: Persistence of High Inflation and High Unemployment*. Federal Reserve Bank of Boston.

Fudenberg, D., and J. Tirole. 1983. "Sequential Bargaining with Incomplete Information." *Review of Economic Studies* 50:221–248.

Grandmont, J. M., and Y. Younes. 1973. "On the Efficiency of a Monetary Equilibrium." *Review of Economic Studies* 40:149–165.

Hart, O. D. 1982. "A Model of Imperfect Competition with Keynesian Features." *Quarterly Journal of Economics* 97:109–138.

Kahneman, D., P. Slovic, and A. Tversky, eds. 1982. *Judgment under Uncertainty: Heuristics and Biases*. Cambridge: Cambridge University Press.

Lancaster, T. 1979. "Econometric Methods for the Duration of Unemployment." *Econometrica* 47:939–956.

References

Loikkanen, H. 1982. "Housing Demand and Intra-Urban Mobility Decisions: A Search Approach." *Commentationes Scientiarum Socialium* 17/1982, Societas Scientiarum Fennica.

Lucas, R. 1972. "Expectations and the Neutrality of Money." *Journal of Economic Theory* 4:103–124; reprinted in his *Studies in Business Cycle Theory,* Cambridge, Massachusetts: MIT Press, 1981.

Lucas, R. 1981. "Rules, Discretion and the Role of the Economic Adviser." In *Studies in Business Cycle Theory,* Cambridge, Massachusetts: MIT Press.

Lucas, R., and E. Prescott. 1974. "Equilibrium Search and Unemployment." *Journal of Economic Theory* 7:188–209.

Lucas, R., and T. Sargent. 1981. *Rational Expectations and Econometric Practice.* Minneapolis: University of Minnesota Press.

Macaulay, S. 1963. "Non-Contractual Relations in Business: A Preliminary Study." *American Sociological Review* 28:55–67.

MacNeil, I. 1974. "The Many Futures of Contract." *Southern California Law Review* 47:691–816.

Mankiw, G., J. Rotemberg, and L. Summers. Forthcoming. "Intertemporal Substitution in Macroeconomics." *Quarterly Journal of Economics.*

Marvel, H. 1976. "The Economics of Information and Retail Gasoline Price Behavior: An Empirical Analysis." *Journal of Political Economy* 84:1033–1060.

Mortensen, D. 1982a. "The Matching Process as a Noncooperative Bargaining Game." In *The Economics of Information and Uncertainty*, edited by J. J. McCall, Chicago: University of Chicago Press.

Mortensen, D. 1982b. "Property Rights and Efficiency in Mating, Racing, and Related Games." *American Economic Review* 72:968–979.

Myrdal, G. 1956. *Development and Underdevelopment*. National Bank of Egypt Fiftieth Anniversary Commemoration Lectures, Cairo.

Nickell, S. 1979. "Estimating the Probability of Leaving Unemployment." *Econometrica* 47:1249–1266.

Nisbett, R., and L. Ross. 1980. *Human Inference: Strategies and Shortcomings of Social Judgment*. Englewood Cliffs, New Jersey: Prentice-Hall.

Okun, A. 1980. "Rational-Expectations-with-Misperceptions as a Theory of the Business Cycle." *Journal of Money, Credit and Banking* 12 (no. 4, pt. 2): 817–825.

Okun, A. 1981. *Prices and Quantities: A Macroeconomic Analysis*. Washington, D. C.: The Brookings Institution.

References

Phelps, E. S., ed. 1970. *The Microeconomic Foundations of Employment and Inflation Theory.* New York: W. W. Norton.

Phelps, E. S., and J. Taylor. 1977. "Stabilizing Powers of Monetary Policy." *Journal of Political Economy* 85:63–90.

Pratt, J., D. Wise, and R. Zeckhauser. 1979. "Price Differences in Almost Competitive Markets." *Quarterly Journal of Economics* 93:189–212.

Reinganum, J. 1979. "A Simple Model of Equilibrium Price." *Journal of Political Economy* 87:851–858.

Salop, S., and J. Stiglitz. 1982. "A Theory of Sales: A Simple Model of Equilibrium Price Dispersion with Identical Agents." *American Economic Review* 72:1121–1130.

Sargent, T., and N. Wallace. 1975. "Rational Expectations, the Optimal Monetary Instrument, and the Optimal Money Supply Rate." *Journal of Political Economy* 83:241–254.

Shiller, R. 1978. "Rational Expectations and the Dynamic Structure of Macroeconomic Models: A Critical View." *Journal of Monetary Economics* 4:1–44.

Solow, R. 1978. "What We Know and Don't Know about Inflation." *Technology Review* 81:2–18.

"Symposium on Rational Expectations in Microeconomic Models." 1982. *Journal of Economic Theory* 26:201–351.

Tobin J. 1980. *Asset Accumulation and Economic Activity.* Chicago: University of Chicago Press.

Wicksell Lectures 1958–1975

The future of the European payments system
Robert Triffin (1958)

Patterns of trade and development
Ragnar Nurkse (1959)

Monetary policy in a mixed economy
A. K. Cairncross (1960)

International payments and monetary policy in the world today
F. A. Lutz (1961)

Stability and growth in the American economy
Paul A. Samuelson (1962)

The European economic community: conservative or progressive?
Jan Tinbergen (1963)

The nature and sources of unemployment in the United States
Robert M. Solow (1964)

Involuntary foreign lending
Fritz Machlup (1965)

The political element in economic development
Andreas Papandreou (1966)

Wicksell Lectures

On the nature of the monetary mechanism
Don Patinkin (1967)

Comparative cost and commercial policy theory for a developing world economy
Harry G. Johnson (1968)

Aspects of tropical trade 1883–1965
W. Arthur Lewis (1969)

Growth, cycles, and exchange rates: the experience of West Germany
Herbert Giersch (1970)

Environmental protection, international spillovers, and trade
William J. Baumol (1971)

Political economy of stability in Western countries
Carl C. von Weizsäcker (1972)

Economic mobility and national economic policy
Richard N. Cooper (1973)

Soviet postwar economic development
Abram Bergson (1974)

The economics of technological change
Poul Nørregaard Rasmussen (1975)